Talk to me like
I'm a human

*Musings and ponderings on
workplace communications,
generations, and connecting*

From the mind of Pat Fontana

Special thanks to Fred Fontana and Sharon Lind

Cover graphics by Durand Mitchell

Edited by Michael LaRocca

Inside graphics by Daniel Bipes and Pixabay

©2019 WordsWorking. All rights reserved

ISBN 978-0-359-42481-8

www.words-working.net

Wilmington NC

No texting at the table

Words for good

In the virtual world, remember the humans!

Who?

You need to read this book if you:

- Are an **employee** searching for ways to improve your communication skills at work (and maybe even at home!)
- Are a **manager** who wants to be more effective in your leadership skills, particularly when developing your team
- Are a **business owner** ready to grow your organization by communicating in a more meaningful (and human) way with clients and within your organization.

Sound like you? Read on ....

Why?

Yes, of course we are all humans. Duh. But, how often do we communicate like humans? How much more often do we let our electronics do the talking, as we text or tweet or message each other?

More importantly, how often do we forget that there are actual humans on the other end of those electronic messages?

Can't solve all the world's problems here, but hopefully we can do something to change the way people in the workplace communicate with ...

wait for it ...

other people.

Ta da! That's the issue. There are actually other people, right there with you, across the conference table or across the desk.

And, of course, there are real people reading those words you send flying through cyberspace on your electronic device. Remember that before you hit "post" or "send."

Ok, no lectures. Just some guidance, some questions, and some reminders. We all started out learning how to talk and write to actual humans. Let's just take a bit of time to go back to those basics and learn (re-learn?) how to communicate like a human!

Introduction – really, you want to read this one

Yeah, I know. I normally don't read Introductions either. But now that you're here, it'll be worth your time to stay and read a page or two.

For one, you'll get an explanation about this book. It's not your normal book on communications. It's a compilation of thoughts, advice, solid information, and (to be honest) pure opinion.

Everything within these pages is based on actual experience. Too much time spent in the classroom (as an instructor) and in the boardroom (as a training manager) will generate lots of experiences. That's good news for you, though. You have the opportunity to gain without all the pain!

How does communication affect you? It's in everything you do. If you own a business, you have to communicate with your employees, your customers, and other business owners. If you are one of those employees, you also have to communicate with team members and managers. And, you have to know how to do it right.

Most business people think about communication in terms of what to say and when to say it. However, what NOT to say and when to STOP saying it are just as important.

Emails that ramble on and on, introductions that give your life story, and office conversations that have people making excuses to leave the room can be killer communications. I've actually read articles giving advice on how to get rid of someone who stops by your office to "chat" and overstays his or her welcome. Do you want to be that "someone"?

And then there are meetings. Ugh. The necessary evil of the business world, meetings actually can be effective. There have to be some new rules, though.

No electronics allowed in the meeting HAS to be one of those new rules. Don't you want everyone paying attention to the topic and the people in the room, instead of to their virtual worlds? Trust me, the meeting will have so much more meaning if everyone puts down their electronic device ... at least long enough to have a real conversation with the real people in the room.

If you are a business person, hopefully you have customers or clients. If you do, you need to know how to communicate with them. Your staff needs to be able to communicate with them.

Let's go back to the basics of manners. "Please" and "thank you" carry so much weight. Look up, focus on your customer, and practice your manners. Get rid of "here you go" and blank stares.

We are so bogged down with clichés in the business world, but here's one more:

Communication IS key. It IS the driver of your success.

Learn how to do it right. Know what to say and when to say it, but just as importantly, what not to say and when to stop saying it. I can't promise the sun will shine a little brighter, but I can tell you that your business will be better off for it. Your employees and your customers will appreciate you more.

Oh, and there may be some repetition in the following. It is essentially a series of essays and short articles. We learn best by repetition, though, don't we? I imagine there is a rule about the number of exposures needed to have a point soak in, although I can't remember it at the moment. I'll have to do some pondering on that! Keep reading for the answer.

Hang on and keep up. There are a lot of bits and pieces here on many different aspects of workplace communications. They're all connected. They're connected by the fact that you always – *always* – communicate with humans, regardless of the method, mode, place, or situation.

As you read through these tips and thoughts, remember:

> *I am your customer or vendor. I am human.*

> *I am your co-worker. I am human.*

> *I am your boss or your employee. I am human.*

Yes, even if you think some of the people in your workplace just landed from Mars, we are all, in reality, human.

So ... talk to me like I'm a human. The workplace – and the world – will be a better place.

◻ ◻ ◻

"The void created by the failure to communicate is soon filled with poison, drivel and misrepresentation."

~ C. Northcote Parkinson

NO TEXTING
AT THE TABLE

What is the power of the unplugged word?

Have you ever misinterpreted an email or text – or worse yet, not received the message at all – and decided that the sender must be mad at you? Have you sent countless messages back and forth, trying to clarify the intent or content of the original message?

We lose so much when all we see are words on a screen. We cannot hear the voice, note the body language, or maintain eye contact with the person on the other end. We quite often determine for ourselves the emotions and the intent behind the message. And we quite often are wrong.

The unplugged word carries the power of empathy, of listening, of feedback and focused response, none of which are possible through texting, emailing, tweeting, or any other form of electronic communication.

Technology can be a good thing, of course, when used appropriately. We use a piece of technology to make a phone call. In that phone call, though, we can hear – and relay back – emotions and intent.

Customer service reps are taught to smile on every call because that cheerfulness will come through in the rep's voice even when the smile can't be seen. Anger, happiness, confusion, and clarity are all quite evident in a caller's voice, leaving little room for misinterpretation or miscommunication.

Unplugged words are spoken face-to-face and on those calls. Unplugged words carry the power of true communication, from one human to another.

Is it a generational thing?

Flappers, Hippies, and . . . Millennials

"We are the Younger Generation. The war tore away our spiritual foundations and challenged our faith. We are struggling to regain our equilibrium."

This was written in 1922, by a "flapper" named Ellen Welles Page. It would certainly hold true again if written by a hippie in the late 60s and early 70s, or if written by one of today's young Millennials or GenZers. Although we don't think of Millennials and GenZers as being radicals, they are certainly of a different mindset and are shaking up the business world as we know it.

Young people always want to change the world. When Boomers were hippies, they (we) saw the world from a vastly different perspective, one that could not trust anyone over 30. Now that they (we) are hovering around double that age, we wonder what is wrong with these young kids today. The truth is, they are just like us. In fact, they are mostly like they are because of the way we raised them.

Flappers were essentially women who just wanted to be comfortable. They wore new hairstyles and clothing that was far less rigid and "proper" than their mothers and grandmothers thought was appropriate. They developed their own language.

Hippies wore new hairstyles and clothing that their parents did not think proper. They developed their own language.

Millennials are trying to find their way in a corporate world that doesn't fit them well. They developed their own language.

Generation gaps exist whenever a new generation approaches the age where they can speak up, have a voice, and be a factor in the world, particularly the business world. The greatest generation gaps have occurred in the 1920s, 1960s and early 70s, and today. How do we communicate with people who are so far from us, in age and in mindset?

We have to consider not only the mode of communication but the content as well. It's no secret that everything is electronic in the world of the Millennial and the GenZer. They don't understand why everyone can't just text or tweet or communicate through social media. Older generations can't understand why the younger set can't just pick up a phone or sit in a face-to-face meeting. Beyond that, though, the language itself is different. And it will always be different.

What we have today is an extreme version of the generation gap, mostly because of the exponential speed of technological developments. However, it is a gap that can be bridged, with a little effort and a lot of understanding. Kids today are not simply trying to be belligerent; rather, they are trying to make the world their own, just as the flappers and the hippies did so many years ago.

In 1922, the flapper added: "I want to beg all you parents, and grandparents, and friends, and teachers, and preachers—you who constitute the 'older generation'—to overlook our shortcomings, at least for the present, and to appreciate our virtues."

Let's take the time to understand all of the generations in the workplace today, including the newest Generation Z that will soon be a factor as well. We can bridge this gap . . . and the workplace will be a better place for it.

The fifth generation

"Each generation imagines itself to be more intelligent than the one that went before it, and wiser than the one that comes after it."
~George Orwell

16- to 20-year-olds are now taking on after school and even full-time jobs, bringing a fifth generation to the already complicated and challenging multi-generational workplace. Those 16-year-olds could quite possibly find themselves working with the 76-year-olds who have delayed retirement. They will certainly be side-by-side with or reporting to the three generations in between.

The oldest group of these workers, including those 76-year-olds, is referred to as Traditionalists or the Silent Generation. They are called this because they believe in loyalty to company and boss. They were raised to do what they were told, to appreciate what they have, and to focus on moving up within their own organization rather than jumping ship for new opportunities.

The next generation is called the Baby Boomers, as they are the generation that was born beginning right after the end of World War II, when soldiers were coming home and starting families in droves. Until very recently, this was the largest generation in the workplace.

This group has experienced a lot of change in their lifetimes and is actually the group that caused the Great Generation Gap in the 1960s and 70s, with a firm belief that no one over 30 could be trusted.

A kind of neglected and lost generation is Generation X. They are the smallest in number, who experienced a number of firsts. They were the first latchkey kids, with both parents working for the first time, and the first to experience a high rate of divorce among their parents.

This group was the start of the "everybody gets a trophy" mentality, quite possibly because their parents felt guilty about not being home for them.

Then there are the Millennials, the group that is replacing the Baby Boomers as the largest force in the workplace. Eyes roll and words like "entitled" roll off the tongue of the previous generations when this group is mentioned.

Born and bred in technology, members of this generation generally have a different way of looking at work, at time, and at personal space.

The fifth generation has been labeled Generation Z. They are also being called the New Silent Generation, because they use their phones to text and tweet and do everything but actually speak.

They prefer to message rather than talk, even if their message recipient is sitting right next to them. This is the group that is starting to come into the workforce and quite possibly, along with the Millennials before them, change the employment environment drastically.

Generations have always clashed, as the younger ones believe they have a firmer grasp on reality than their elders and the more senior generations believe they are so much wiser than the youth could possibly ever be. The flappers of the 1920s, the hippies of the 1960s, and now the technology-dependent Millennials and New Silent Generation clash with their elders, but that may not necessarily be such a bad thing.

Youth always want to change the world. They also want to change the workplace now. Why should they sit in a cubicle and work 9 to 5, in a virtual world that operates 24/7? Why should they take the time to schedule a meeting and have in-person conversations when they can whip out a text or a tweet and have that communication happen instantaneously?

Communicating across generations is a challenge for many in the workplace. The key to effective communication is always to consider the receiver.

To break down the perceived barriers and work toward better communications with the five generations now in the workplace, take the time to understand each generation better.

Where are they coming from?

Where do they want to go?

What method should I use – and when should I use it – to make sure my message is understood?

It will take some work on all sides, but the gap can be narrowed, if not completely closed.

There will always be a generation gap

New generations come along roughly every 18-20 years. Each new generation brings with it . . . well, let's just say "challenges" . . . for existing generations.

Those challenges are most clearly evident in the realm of workplace communications.

Communication technology has advanced us eons from where we were just a few short years ago. Baby Boomers (and beyond) probably still remember their first exciting, although bulky and cumbersome, computer. Who knew that only a few decades later, computers that used to fill a room would fit on a wristwatch?

Of course, Millennials (and beyond) have always known that computers should be small enough to fit on a phone or a wristwatch. Anything else is certainly an antique.

So how do these widely varying groups get together to communicate effectively in the workplace?

The answer, which takes some effort on all sides, is three-part: commonalities, consideration, and compromise.

Commonalities

Tossing the generalities and stereotypes aside for the moment, let's look at the most important aspect of the answer: commonalities. We all work with people from different generations, different backgrounds, different experiences. That's what makes a lot of workplaces interesting and effective. However, it's also a contributing factor to communication challenges, particularly among those caught in the generation gap.

What are the commonalities we can tap into, when attempting to communicate across generations? For one, the very fact that we need to communicate is common among all involved. We all need to be informed, to share information, and to be "in the loop." Lack of communication in the workplace is a major factor in employee frustration and discontent.

Another commonality is that most of us prefer to communicate using a mode with which we are most comfortable. Older generations tend to appreciate face-to-face or telephone conversations more. Younger generations feel the need for speed and immediacy, so they tend to turn to their smartphones or some other form of virtual communication. When we are comfortable with the mode, the theory goes, the communication itself will be more successful.

Consideration

The second part of the answer, consideration, involves understanding not just our own comfort zone but, more importantly, the comfort zone of our communication audience. One of the first lessons we learn about communication is that it does no good if the recipient is not able to process the information. Who is on the receiving end of your message? How do they most effectively process a piece of communication? News flash: it's not all about you. Consider the recipient to make your communication effort truly successful.

Compromise

That leads us to the final part of the answer: compromise. When communicating across generations, stop and think about your intended recipient. If that person prefers to speak on the phone, do not continue to send him emails or text messages. Your communication may well go into a virtual black hole. If the recipient prefers brief messages that get to the point immediately, do not send her several paragraphs that she has to wade through to find the real message. She won't bother to read past the first line and your message will also be lost.

There will always be a generation gap, particularly in regard to communications. If we take a few moments, though, and look for commonalities, consider our audience, and compromise on the mode of communication, we might all just be a little more successful at bridging that gap.

Generational communication is a five-way street

The young intern wants to text everyone or communicate via social media. The senior executive wants face-to-face meetings and telephone conversations. The middle manager insists that all information be emailed. Attempts to communicate across generations can hit roadblocks at every turn. With five generations in the workplace now, the communication process must be a five-way street.

Each generation brings with it new ways and new ideas, and new opportunities for older generations to question what these new kids are doing and why. The younger generation, in turn, doesn't understand why the older groups stick to their antiquated ways. And the clash begins.

The youngest generation, Generation Z, now joins the four other generations working together in the business world. Throughout history, each new generation has shared a culture, an upbringing, and experiences that make them different from their predecessors. Technological advances, wars, economic struggles, and family values all influence the way each generation thinks – and the way each generation prefers to communicate.

We shake our heads (smh) and laugh out loud (lol) at the differences in the younger generations coming into the workforce, but there is a good chance that our parents and grandparents had the same reaction to us, only without the text language to accompany it.

Differences seem more pronounced in today's business world, as the rate of technological advances has increased dramatically over the past few years.

Not so long ago, email was the great new communication tool and many Boomers and Gen Xers still cling to it as their preferred method. Younger generations see email as too slow; they need instant responses. The oldest generation in the workplace still prefers to look people in the eye when they communicate, or at least hear their voice.

When the generations clash head-on, it's time for every generation to learn how to yield. When the young intern can't understand why everyone doesn't communicate via text, she needs to step aside and see the senior manager's preference for using the phone as a verbal communication tool. He, in turn, needs to yield to the younger generations' preferences for using their phones only as texting or emailing tools.

Understanding each generation's preferences – and understanding why they are preferences – can help all the generations yield when it comes to communication.

Stop and think before sending a text or picking up the phone and calling. Will the person on the receiving end of the message actually receive it and understand it? Many young people do not have voicemail set up on their phones because they know they will not check it. Some older people have a difficult time with texts.

The mode of communication and the content can vary greatly. Not every Traditionalist will understand when to expect to see you again, after receiving a message that simply says brb. Spell it out and explain that you will "be right back."

These are sweeping generalizations, of course, and there are certainly exceptions, but it is best to know for sure before attempting to communicate in a way that will not be well received.

Communication runs more effectively in all directions when each generation does not simply plow full speed ahead with its own preferred method, but instead stops and yields the road to gain a better understanding of all five generations in the workplace.

And the secret for everyone, of course, is to remember the human on the other end. Even GenZers, clinging to their instant electronic communication system, have to consider how those messages will be received by real humans.

Your turn

(Yes, you're allowed to write in the book!)

What are your challenges when communicating with other generations?

Do you grumble about "kids today" or about the older generation that just doesn't get technology the way you do?

What are some steps you can take to reach those other generations?

Identify how you will:

Find commonalities

Show consideration

Compromise

□ □ □

Need to communicate?

Who, me?

Communication-itis got you down?

Do you recognize the common symptoms of communication-itis?

- You struggle with putting words together to make a sentence
- You stress over what to capitalize, where to put the comma, when to end a sentence
- You're not sure if the word is "your" or "you're"
- You're not sure if the word is "is" or "are"
- You put everything you know into one email
- You put only a few lines in an email and expect the reader to figure out the rest
- The thought of having to write an email terrifies you
- Fear of the blank page is a very real struggle for you

If you recognize these symptoms in yourself, don't despair. There is hope!

The first step is recognizing that you have a problem. So many business owners, marketers, middle managers, and others tasked with communicating on behalf of their business just don't get it. They send out emails, they post articles or blogs, or they lay in web content that is simply unreadable.

Unreadable writing gives potential customers their first impression of you. Do you know how long it takes to develop that first impression? Seconds. How many times do you get a chance to make a positive first impression? One. Do the math. Everything needs to be perfect – i.e., readable – the first time, or there will be no second time.

The next step is to get help. If you struggle with communication-itis, you are most definitely not alone. Many people did not learn what they needed to in kindergarten or fourth grade or even high school. Fortunately, there are also many ways to make up that education deficit. Hire a freelance writer or take a class in business writing.

Proofreading and securing the assistance of a second set of eyes can also help you. If you're not sure what you're looking for when you proofread, ask someone else to read your written piece. It's a known scientific fact that writers only see what they want to see when proofreading their own work.

If you're not sure you have communication-itis, a second set of eyes can also set you straight on that issue. The person belonging to those eyes may need to tread carefully, of course, depending on your relationship. Just remember that whatever feedback you're given, it's for your own good.

If you have communication-itis, it can affect your business in many ways. By the way, there's another symptom: would you have known to use "affect" in the previous sentence and not "effect"?

Effective, appropriate, well-written communication is essential for a healthy business. Take care of your communication-itis, before it affects your business!

Are communication issues costing your organization?

Do you have workplace communication issues?

If you do, would you know it?

What is miscommunication – or lack of communication – costing your organization?

If you think weekly staff meetings or hourly emails count as effective communication, you might want to take a closer look at the results, if any, you are seeing from those strategies.

Weekly staff meetings are a waste of time if your staff is more concerned about keeping in touch with those outside the room than with paying attention to the discussion inside the room. Consider implementing a "no texting at the table" policy. Then, communicate something worthy of their attention in each and every meeting!

Poorly written emails quite often require follow-up and further explanations. Subtleties such as humor and sarcasm are frequently misinterpreted. It's crucial to know when to email and when to have an actual, face-to-face (or phone) conversation.

How do you know if you have communication issues? Look around.

- Do employees rely on rumor rather than fact?
- Are your customers in the dark?
- Are your meeting participants focused on their electronic devices instead of the people in the room?
- Do you spend excessive amounts of time clarifying details with customers, employees, or vendors?

Think about it. Not communicating well – or, worse, not communicating at all – can create major issues within your organization. Miscommunication or lack of communication can cost you valued customers, quality employees, work contracts . . . all of which can lead to financial costs. In severe cases, where health and safety are concerned, communication issues can have much more devastating costs.

Think about it. Then act on it. A communication plan, including training for staff and management, can prove to be a worthwhile investment of your time and money. A plan that includes real communication with real people can help your staff get back in touch with each other, with management, and with your clients. By putting aside or at least limiting the use of electronic devices and emphasizing the need for a real conversation, you will reduce misunderstandings and build relationships.

Communication issues can cost your organization more than you may realize. Reconnect with a solid communication plan and with quality, customized training for your organization.

5 signs of communication issues in your workplace

Do you know the signs of miscommunication in the workplace? Are you satisfied with the regular meetings you have with your staff or emails you send to clients? Do you recognize certain challenges as being a direct result of communication issues in your workplace? Here are five signs that you might have communication issues in your workplace.

Employee morale declines

What do employees do when managers don't communicate with them? They get discouraged, feel less valued, and begin to make up their own versions of the facts (better known as rumors). In an organization that is dominated by upper management meetings, with very little information being distributed from those meetings to staff members, morale declines. Employees feel they are not important enough to receive the information they need. Those rumors swirl. Employees leave.

Lengthy explanations are required

Here's a trick question: how many times do you send emails to someone who didn't understand – or misconstrued – the first one? Emails are prone to misinterpretation by their very nature. Body language, tone of voice, sarcasm, humor . . . all are lost in the plain black and white of simple words being transmitted electronically. If you and your staff find yourselves continuously following up on emails that require lengthy explanations to be understood, your organization has a communication issue.

Clients are confused and frustrated

Along the same lines, if your clients frequently require follow-up explanations of your communication efforts, your organization has a communication issue. Have you had clients call or email or show up on your doorstep, trying to get more information? Are they frustrated that no one called them or provided them with the latest news about your products or services? Have you ever had a client say they found out about something through social media, rather than directly from your organization? Clients who are confused and frustrated also leave.

Internal meetings are a waste of time

You pride yourself on conducting regular internal meetings, so your staff stays informed. That's a good start. However, how often do those meetings turn into a waste of time for the participants, including you? Does the conversation often get sidetracked? Do you spend a lot of time discussing issues that are not on the agenda? Do sidebars distract everyone in the meeting, to the point where the sidebar is more interesting (and gathers more attention) than the primary topic of discussion? Do you and your staff walk away from these meetings with a sense of accomplishment or a sense of relief that you don't have to go through that again for another week?

Employees don't have the information they need to do their job properly

When your team can't do its job properly, the entire organization suffers. Employees walk. Clients walk. Enough said.

Your turn

Take a look around your workplace. What issues do you see that are a direct result of miscommunication or misinterpretation?

How many times do you go back and forth trying to clarify emails? Seriously, count them.

Are your customers saying you don't communicate well with them? (Hint: that would be a great first sign of the need for better communication strategies.)

Pick up the phone and make a call or walk down the hall and have a real conversation with customers and team members. How did that work out for you and for them?

□ □ □

Yes, your customers do notice

The customer service – communication connection

We've all encountered less than stellar customer service. The fast food worker gets the order wrong and doesn't seem to care. The call center rep is obviously reading from a script and can't actually help you with your unique problem. The cashier barely acknowledges you and makes it clear she'd rather be somewhere else.

What do all of these scenarios have in common? Yes, students, you know by now that the answer is . . . communications.

Workplace communications play a significant part in customer service. The quality of external communications is often a reflection of the internal situation. The way employees communicate with each other, and perhaps more importantly, the way managers communicate with employees, can significantly impact the quality of the customer service provided to your customers. Tone of voice, choice of words, and timeliness of conveyance can all affect each communication effort.

Although we think of customer service interactions as being primarily face-to-face or phone conversations, written communications also play a part. If your managers are not able to express themselves effectively via email or written memo to their employees, then the communication efforts fail. If employees cannot properly compose an email or letter to a customer, you may even lose that customer.

A great (or not so great, depending on your point of view) example of the latter happened recently to a man who emailed a car dealership to inquire about a used car he had viewed on their website. The response to the email was not an answer to any of his questions, but rather a form email that was, without a doubt, an automated response.

Within minutes, he received three more form emails, including one that referenced a visit to the dealership's showroom that clearly never happened. That dealership definitely lost a potential customer, solely because of their inept communication efforts.

Proper internal communications can:

- Improve employee morale, so that employees take more pride in their work and actually want to be helpful to customers
- Provide employees with the information they need to be able to help customers, even when the answer is not in the script
- Give customers the assurance that they will get consistent information and assistance from each employee
- Improve employee retention, providing customers the comfort level that they will not have to deal with a new person each time they interact with your organization
- Improve the quality of your organization's customer service efforts, on all levels.

What kind of customer service is your business providing? Are your employees communicating clearly and politely with your customers? Are you communicating in a timely and effective basis with your employees? The connection between the quality of your communications and the quality of your customer service is clear . . . and vital to your organization's success.

There you go . . .
the new language of customer service

Although I have extensive experience educating others and a well-rounded education of my own, I somehow missed the class on Interpreting Customer Service Language. Who knew that "there you go" is now acceptable customer service language for "thanks for your business"? Likewise, a blank stare is apparently now supposed to be translated into "how may I help you?"

Occasionally, I will test this new language by sneering "thank you" after the cashier thrusts my receipt in my hand with a hearty proclamation of "there you go." My overly-subtle sarcasm is obviously totally lost on the poor soul, though, as my intention was to make her realize the error of her communication.

She should be the one thanking me for choosing to spend my hard-earned money at her employer's place of business, right? However, her response to my "thank you" is quite often a very confused "you're welcome."

The philosophy that the customer is always right has also been dropped from the communication section of the Customer Service curriculum. I've had to wait – and I've held up lines behind me waiting – attempting to use a coupon at the grocery store because the store's computer system itself was not communicating properly.

In one instance, in a confrontation that will undoubtedly scar me for life, the cashier stated, "you didn't buy this." She then proceeded to forage through the ten or so bags of groceries she had just rung up, to see if I was pulling a fast one when I asserted that I did, indeed, buy that particular item.

I also asserted my innocence at the implied accusation that I was trying to con the store out of 50 cents. The search continued and I was eventually proven, in fact, to be a customer who was right.

Then there was the staring contest. I was supposed to translate a blank stare emanating from a less than enthusiastic fast food employee standing at a register as "Welcome to my fine burger establishment. May I take your order?"

Instead I decided to try to speak his language and stare back at him. The result was a game of who-will-blink-first. The burgers were not so fine when the transaction was finally completed.

So either I missed the class that would allow me, as a consumer, to understand the new communication style of those charged with providing me customer service – or they missed the class on how to effectively communicate with real people. The spoken word, body language, attitudes, all should be covered in a how-to for people whose livelihood depends on interacting with other people.

Maybe the diagnosis of this growing problem lies in the phrase "communicate with real people." In the 21st century, we have lost the focus on real people, as communication has moved so quickly and drastically into the virtual world. If we can't communicate in 280 characters, in mostly abbreviated forms of what used to be words, we are lost.

In Electronic Communication Land, we can simply delete a conversation we do not like. Not so much, when the person attempting to have the conversation is standing right in front of us.

When electronic communication devices are attached like umbilical cords and virtual communication becomes instantaneous and effortless, real-life communication presents an often insurmountable challenge.

We've entered the Backwards World of communication, especially in situations requiring real customer service language. Perhaps it's not the consumer who needs the interpretation class, after all. Rather, it's time for the customer service world to relearn how to communicate with real customers.

Your turn

Pay attention to your experience as a customer over the next few days. How often do you hear "thank you"? Take note of where and when it occurred.

Over the next week, focus on making sure **your** customers know they are appreciated. Consciously eliminate phrases such as "there you go" and "no problem." Replace them with "please" and "thank you." Note your experiences here.

❏ ❏ ❏

Got words?

You can't center around or be very unique

It's the little things, really. It's quite possible that not everyone even notices those little things. Are you willing to take the chance, though?

What are these little things and why should you be concerned with them, you may ask. The little things are those annoying, potentially minor errors in written and spoken communications that leave the reader or the listener with the impression that you don't really know what you're talking about because you can't even get a simple phrase right. Little things can also cause seriously major issues when you're not communicating effectively or properly.

For example:

Center around: By its very nature, "centering" cannot be around anything. You can center on, but you can't center around. Very similar is the phrase "focus around." Again, by its very nature, focusing has to be directed on something. You cannot focus around a topic. So, if you're attempting to center or focus around, you're clearly unfocused.

Very unique: Really, using any modifier with unique is not appropriate. Unique means one of a kind. How can you be "very one of a kind"? Almost laughable was a recent radio story in which the reporter described someone as "very, very unique." That person was really one of a kind! You can't be a little unique or somewhat unique. You either are or you aren't.

Hot water heater: Okay, most business people don't have a need to discuss a water heater, but if you do (in a networking situation, for example), it is a water heater. The device does not heat hot water; it heats water to make it hot.

Stop light: It's a go light too! Again, not usually used in business conversations but annoying to those in the transportation business. Refer to it as a traffic signal.

Farther / further: You can't explore your career options farther, unless you are physically walking them down the road. Farther is about distance, something measurable. You can discuss a topic further, but you might have to move farther down the hall to talk about it without anyone hearing you. A major car company markets with a tagline of "go further." No clue what they mean by that, since it would seem they would actually want your car to go farther down the road.

The list could most definitely go on (and may well do just that in a future book.)

These may seem like little things, primarily noticeable only by an English major deeply concerned with others' business communications skills, but . . . little things contribute to bigger impressions. And, bigger impressions contribute to your ability to communicate with, and to work with, co-workers, managers, vendors, and customers.

Mind the little things and the bigger impressions will become more respected impressions. Your communication will improve. Your business will improve.

When words are not words

When Baby Boomers were young, we were admonished that "ain't" isn't a word.

But it's in the dictionary, we argued.

It's not proper English, we were told.

Now we have so many more words that are not really words, and the argument over "ain't" seems rather silly.

A word that has become commonplace in speech and (frighteningly) in the written word is "gonna." We do sometimes get lazy when we talk, particularly if we are in an informal conversation with a group of friends, so "I'm gonna do that" will easily slip out. However, I have seen this "word" used in print much too often. Of course, the fact that it is used at all, even once, is too often.

For those of you who are still trying to figure out what the problem is, the actual words are "going to." Gonna ain't a word.

And then there's all the text language. Yes, it has become its own language apparently, as that is the way it is referred to now. It certainly seems like a foreign language to many of us.

It is now acceptable in an informal virtual conversation to state that you will brt. But again, I've had people verbally tell me that they will brt. Is it that difficult to say, I'll "be right there?"

Words that are not words do not belong in professional, workplace communications. Words should be complete and actual words, forming complete and actual sentences. It may take a little effort, spelling out a two-letter word rather than using just the first letter, but with a little practice I'm sure we can master it.

Professional communications must be . . . professional. Too often they are not, mostly because the writer or speaker uses those words that are not words. I often smh at the emails I receive from others in the business world. If it weren't so sad, I might actually lol.

Your turn

Be honest about this one. Do you use words that are not words? List
them here.

Stay honest. Are there words (real words) that give you trouble? What
can you do to resolve that challenge?

Pay attention to written messages you receive, whether in your workplace or from other business people. Are they well written in your opinion? Do you have problems reading and interpreting their message?

❏ ❏ ❏

Lo, the dreaded meeting

No texting at the table

The following suggestion may shock and astound you. It's a new concept, not always easily grasped, especially in the workplace. Those of you who participate in meetings (and that's probably all of you) will have the most difficult time understanding the process. However, if executed properly, this suggestion could change your life considerably.

The earth-shaking suggestion?

Put down your electronic devices, if only for a few minutes!

It will only be temporary. The pain will pass quickly. Stay strong and you will soon notice many positive results.

Your communication skills will improve. Your workplace relationships will improve. You will actually be able to recognize the faces of the people in your workplace.

You've heard (and hopefully used) the phrase "No texting at the table" around the dinner table, to encourage your kids to focus on the family rather than on their electronic devices. The same phrase should be used around the conference table or even just across the desk, to encourage staff to focus on the people in the room and the message being conveyed there.

Take a minute to look around the room during your next staff meeting. Are you the only one looking up? Are the others all engrossed in their smartphones or laptops or pads?

Are they paying attention to the discussion in the room . . . or the virtual discussion on their electronic devices? How confident are you that anything happening in the meeting is actually penetrating the participants' otherwise-occupied brains?

If you're the meeting participant and your face – and your attention – are buried in your electronic device, what does that say to the others around you? That they are less important than the people on the other end of your virtual communication? That they are less important than your web browsing, texting, email responding, or (gasp) game playing?

Too many questions – and definitely not enough good answers.

It's time to try a revolutionary new concept: real communication with real people. Look at the people you're with; talk to the people you're with. Put down your electronic device and have a conversation.

No texting at the table, whether it's the dinner table or the conference table.

Make meetings matter

"What a waste of time."

"Could have just emailed it in."

"Do we have to do this every week?"

Comments from last week's meeting ring in your head as you prepare for today's staff meeting. Will it be the same old, same old? Or will today's meeting actually be a good use of everyone's time? What can you do to keep everyone's attention and get them involved? How can you send them off with motivation and a sense of accomplishment?

Starting today, change it up. Make sure it's not the same old, same old. Make sure your meetings matter.

Before the meeting

Decide whether the meeting is truly necessary and will accomplish specific goals. Set expectations. Assign responsibilities. Invite only those people who literally bring something to the table.

Attendees often think of meetings as free time. If they don't play a role in the meeting, they don't have to pay attention. Review your attendee list carefully. Does everyone have to attend every meeting? If so, give them something to do, to bring, or to report. Involve all of your attendees before the meeting so they will know it's not just another block of free time.

During the meeting

Establish a new rule: No texting at the table. All attendees must focus on what is being said in the room, not on their electronic devices.

How many times have you had to repeat information, either during the meeting or after, because people weren't paying attention to you? Take away their biggest distraction and they will focus on the topic at hand and on the person discussing that topic. They might even join the discussion!

Re-emphasize your key points to summarize the meeting at the end. Ask all attendees to reiterate the tasks they were assigned during the meeting, to ensure they truly understand what was discussed and what is needed from them, including their deadlines.

After the meeting

Follow up. Check in with the attendees in a few days, to see if they are progressing with their assignments or if they need further clarification. Don't wait until the next meeting to find out they've not done anything or were not clear on what they were supposed to do.

The thread that binds

Communicate! Before, during, and after the meeting, communicate clearly and establish expectations for responses. Communication is not complete until the cycle is complete – the receiver must acknowledge that he or she has received and understood the communication.

Get their feedback. Get their attention. Get meetings that matter.

Cut the (virtual) cord – no texting while meeting

Do you fear that if you put your cell phone away long enough to pay attention in a staff meeting, that you'll miss a tweet or a twerp or whatever flows in next through the social media pipeline?

Are the emails coming in at such a furious rate that you would simply never catch up again if you were to put the phone down long enough to have a real conversation with the person across the table from you?

Oh please, don't try to profess your innocence. You know this describes you . . . and your electronic device dependence.

How ironic that the technology of wireless cell phones doesn't require being plugged in to function, yet we as humans can't seem to function now without constantly being plugged in to our phones.

Something might happen in the world that we won't know about instantaneously. We might even have to wait a few minutes to read and respond to a virtual message if we take our eyes (and our thumbs) off the device to look up and across the table.

Texting while driving is a dangerous activity. Don't do it!

Texting while meeting can have its own ramifications. Cut the virtual cord!

It's only temporary. The electronic world will have to wait on you, while you reacquaint yourself with the real people in the room. You can have your phone back if you're good – and if you make a serious effort to interact with the people in the room at your next meeting.

Who knows? You might even experience a new and exciting feeling, brought on by that crazy new activity known as achieving real communications with real people.

No texting at the table. You can do it.

Your turn

Take notice during meetings you participate in or run over the next week. How many of the participants pay more attention to their virtual world than to the people in the room?

During those meetings, does information have to be repeated because people aren't paying attention?

Are there issues after the meetings with participants who are unaware of their assigned responsibilities?

What are some specific steps you can take to make your meetings matter? (Hint: include the rule that no cell phones are allowed.)

□ □ □

Put down the electronic device
and walk slowly away

It's a Pavlov thing . . .

We feel compelled, whenever we hear a bell or a buzz or a beep or some odd snippet of music, to respond. In the 1890s, psychologist Ivan Pavlov discovered through his research that this type of conditioned reflex is not just psychological, but also physiological.

Today, our mind and our body MUST respond to the sounds, as we are physically and mentally connected to our electronic devices.

We panic when we can't find it. We must have it within arm's reach at all times. If asked to silence it or put it aside for the sake of the meeting or the conversation at hand, we stress, worrying that we will miss something of utmost importance coming through the device, something much more important than the people in the room with us.

We are addicted. It's a real thing, this addiction. Cell phone addiction has been the topic of many bona fide research studies. Most come to the same conclusion – we can't put them down. We can't just walk away.

But we must.

In the workplace, we must put down the cell phone – at least when it distracts from the real conversation we need to have with real people. We must have a "no texting at the table" policy that includes "no texting while having a conversation" regardless of where that conversation takes place.

And it's not just a generational thing, as many may believe. How often have we been in meetings where virtually ALL of the participants, regardless of age, are physically and mentally attached to their electronic devices? They may try to be slick, with phones in their laps, texting and surfing on the sly.

Or they might just not care and have the phones out on the table in plain sight, letting everyone know that the conversation they're having online is more important than the conversation in the room.

Isn't it ironic that when we have to be without our phones for even a short amount of time, we feel totally alone and lost – even if we are in a room full of actual, real people? Hey, but guess what? There are actual, real people sitting right across the table from you. You can talk to them! Perhaps even more importantly, you can listen to them! You are not alone!

Talk to them as humans, not as just another electronic device.

No texting at the table – part deux

Everybody talks about the weather, but nobody does anything about it. Whether you believe Mark Twain actually said that (the debate about its origin will be saved for another day), it leaves us with a good point to ponder.

General consensus is that being obsessed with a cell phone is just rude, particularly when there are other real human beings in the room. Articles, letters to advice columnists, and even Dilbert complain about people too focused on their cell phones to have an actual conversation. So why don't we do something about it?

Put it down. Walk away.

Yeah, that won't work. It's like telling a little boy to put down his slimy, squirmy frog and go read a book.

Back to real life. Everybody talks about the irritations of texting at the table, but nobody does anything about it.

Meetings are futile attempts to communicate vital information to the tops of attendees' heads as they are face down in their phones. The place setting for a meal now consists of the plate, silverware, and the cell phone.

Every gathering starts with "please silence your electronic devices," an admonition that, of course, no one hears because they are focused on . . . you got it . . . their electronic devices.

The rant could go on, and it probably will.

Of course technology is a wonderful thing. Electronic devices definitely have their place. Anywhere that live human beings are attempting interpersonal communication, though, is not that place.

How do we "do something about it?" Relearn that process of interpersonal communication. Go off-site, unplug for just a bit, and TALK to each other. What a concept, right?

Find a pen and a piece of paper and write a letter. Or at the very least, jot a few words on a card, offering someone a note of thanks or encouragement – in your own handwriting.

Practice a "no texting at the table" policy at work, at home, in a restaurant, at the coffee shop, anywhere that other people expect to see your full face and expect you to actually talk to them.

Who knows? You might start to recognize some faces for a change, instead of just seeing the tops of your co-workers' heads. For the most part, that will probably be a good thing.

No texting at the table. Put the electronic device down. Forget the frog. Go read a book.

Text neck – really

Let me begin with a statement of fact and of opinion – technology is awesome. The capabilities available today on computers, cell phones, tablets, and all electronic devices are absolutely, without a doubt, incredibly beneficial and almost essential.

Now, that being said . . . put down the electronic device and walk slowly away . . . .

Text neck is a real thing

It turns out that excessive use of our cell phones is not just bad for our interpersonal communications, but it is also bad for our health. Yes, there really is a thing called "text neck." And yes, it is apparently a fairly serious problem.

Too much bending, with our heads down, obsessively focused on our cell phones, can hurt us. Who knew?

Text neck happens when the neck is stretched and stressed more than nature meant it to be. Much more. The muscles in the neck have to do a lot more work when the head is bent excessively, focused on the virtual world. The spine can even be damaged, from the strain caused by the texting neck.

Neck pain and headaches ensue, all because we had to check those texts, tweet those messages, and play those games.

Lots of lamenting

Besides the medical advice, the signs are everywhere that we need to put the devices down and step back when it's appropriate.

Technology is awesome, absolutely. But, our obsession with virtual technology has us drifting too far away from being real people using real communications.

Articles and posts consistently lament the overuse of electronic devices on a daily basis. The authors of these pieces agree that there is a place and a time for electronic device use – and many places and times where it is not welcomed.

It seems we cannot even pick up the telephone and use it as, well, a telephone anymore. We even need an app for ordering pizza.

And it's definitely not a generational thing. Kids and grandmas alike can be seen in the stores, at work, at family gatherings, developing their own text necks. They are not looking at each other. Check it out next time you're around people. Any people, really. Can you see their eyes? Or just the tops of their heads?

What to do?

Put it down. Walk away. Try it, just for a few minutes at least.

Do something different for a while.

Look up. See what's around you. See who's around you. See their faces. Talk to them.

Write a real letter. Take a piece of paper and a pen and create something that will last longer than a text message or a tweet.

Reacquaint yourself with the real world. The virtual world will still be there when your break is over. You, too, can prevent text neck. You might even improve your communications skills along the way.

No texting at the table. Seriously.

Disconnecting to Reconnect

You hear it every day. You've probably even said it more than once. "How rude of people to be on their cell phones while we're trying to talk . . . or meet . . . or have a family meal."

Or maybe you're the one they're talking about, who checks social media whenever you have a few minutes of down time; who has your face buried in your cell phone at meetings, on dates, at family gatherings; who is obsessed with your virtual world, oblivious to the real people around you.

The issue is a major concern on the streets, in the media, and in the boardroom, and a local communications training business is working to help address it.

NPR's All Tech Considered recognized the issue. Their staff participated in an experiment to determine whether reducing their cell phone usage could have positive results. One participant stated that because she reduced her cell phone usage, she "looked up" and noticed that others were also looking up. The general consensus was that it was beneficial to disconnect occasionally.

Another study among Facebook users has found that mindlessly surfing, to fill any available down time, actually impedes mental sharpness.

A CNBC article from 2013 cites employers' frustrations with their workers being unable to communicate effectively. "In survey after survey, employers are complaining about job candidates' inability to speak and write clearly." Most blame an obsession with technology.

Ironically, being constantly connected presents communication challenges for many businesses. Team members are distracted by their virtual world and are not focused on the real people in the room. They have not "looked up" and noticed the other meeting participants, including their own customers.

Let's now focus on developing the essentials of communication that cannot be found on an electronic device. Talking to others like the humans they are resolves a long list of workplace challenges, enabling business people to reconnect through real conversation or clearer written communications, to reduce or eliminate misinterpretation, and to be more effective with their words.

Put down the electronic device, look up, and gain a better understanding of what it means to really communicate with co-workers, employees, managers, vendors, and customers. Believe it or not, they're all humans!

Your turn

How long can you survive without the virtual world? Test it this week. When you need to communicate with a human, put it down and look up. Have a face-to-face conversation. If you need to, use the phone as an actual phone and make a call.

Record your efforts here. Note the difference in the quality of your communications.

"The basic building block of good communications is the feeling that every human being is unique and of value."

~Unknown

Words for good

RUMORS: Infiltrating your organization?

What are **RUMORS**? Rumors are much more destructive than gossip, much more intense than chatter. Rumors infiltrate your organization when:

Real communication does not take place.

Unbelievable stories proliferate.

Managers do not share information with employees.

Overreactions ensue among employees and clients.

Relationships with clients suffer . . .

Sending a message that communication is not important.

How can rumors be stopped? The solution is incredibly simple. Take the time to communicate frequently, at all levels.

Picture the scene: Managers huddle together in a conference room, discussing hot topics such as the future of the project, employee responsibilities, and client expectations. They leave the conference room, return to their desks, and send emails to each other to discuss further the topics that pertain to them in particular. What's missing in this picture?

If you answered that the missing piece is the managers speaking to their employees, you win. Or maybe you lose, because you know from experience what's missing.

If no one is told anything, guess what they do? They make it up as they go along!

Too many top-level business executives feel their employees don't have a need to know certain things. That type of thinking simply exacerbates the culture of rumors. If employees are not given the information they need, they will come to their own conclusions.

Another scene: Managers gather in the conference room, discussing potential layoffs because of a pending merger. They leave the conference room, drawn faces betraying the topic they just discussed, even though they were all told to "keep it in the room." They are not allowed to discuss the situation with their employees.

Most employees are not stupid. They will figure out something is wrong. When it becomes obvious that the information will not – or cannot – be discussed with them, they will fear the worst and make up stories to fit that fear. They do this not because they like to gossip, but because they need dialogue. When communication doesn't happen, rumors become that dialogue.

Rumors lead to decreased employee morale and that will also be reflected in their interactions with clients. As a customer yourself, how many times have you had an organization's employee say to you, "I don't know. They don't tell us anything."

Rumors lead to the loss of clients. Your clients will hear the rumors, or make up their own, when they don't receive the information they need directly from the people who should be providing it. Do your clients learn about important corporate decisions when they read about them in the news? Do they ask employees questions that the employees cannot respond to, because they've not been given the answers?

Instead of RUMORS, try FACTS:

Focus on understanding employees' and clients' need for dialogue.

Act to ensure employees and clients have the information they need.

Clarify misunderstandings immediately so they won't fester.

Talk to employees and clients regularly, in a straightforward manner . . .

Saving business relationships and maybe even the business itself.

Stop the rumors. Communicate.

Responsive or rude?

Overheard in a meeting: "I can't stand it when people reply to an email just to say 'thank you' for something I sent them."

Really? Why would you not want to hear the magic words, "please" and "thank you"? Manners are so important in business communications.

Basic manners should also tell you that you do need to respond to emails. Even if it's just a simple "thank you," that acknowledgement is essential. Being responsive reflects on your image as a business person and on your business as a whole. If you are a job seeker, that "thank you" becomes even more important and can often set you apart from the pack in the hiring process.

So why would someone think it rude to receive a "thank you" email? That person (this one happened to be a man) would appear to be overwhelmed with emails and therefore unappreciative of a short note acknowledging his own email.

Would it not be ruder, though, not to acknowledge a message? If you were sending some crucial information to a colleague or a client and did not get a response, what would be your thoughts? You would either wonder if the email ever reached its intended recipient or maybe decide that the recipient was indeed too rude to take thirty seconds to hit "reply" and type "thank you."

It takes very little effort to choose to use manners in business communication.

Following up after meeting someone is another critical aspect of being responsive. Why do you go to a networking meeting? Certainly it's not to collect more business cards. You are trying to make connections through these gatherings. A connection may be made on the initial contact, but it is reinforced in the follow-up.

Send an email. Handwrite (gasp!) a note. Say "it was a pleasure" or some such manners-centric phrase. If you don't follow up, your business card will be filed and forgotten.

Again, job seekers take note. Follow up! Say "thank you" for the interview. Say you appreciate being considered. Ask the interviewer to "please" contact you with next steps.

Emails do runneth over in this digital age. Even so, you still need to take the time to be responsive. Maybe your recipient will be annoyed by yet another "thank you" email. More than likely, though, your recipient will think you were raised right and will be impressed by your business communication manners.

Why am I the one saying "thank you"?

As a customer, did you feel appreciated when you chose to spend your money in certain stores?

As a business person, do you and your team show appreciation to your customers?

Sure, there might be pleasant utterances such as "have a nice day," but how many times do you hear or do you say … "thank you"?

How often are the words "there you go" uttered instead, when a receipt or shopping bag was handed over?

Is it easier to say "there you go" than "thank you"?

There you go … 3 syllables

Thank you … 2 syllables

Maybe my math is off, but doesn't "thank you" take less effort? It certainly carries greater weight! Think about the warm fuzzy feeling you get when you hear those words. That's the feeling your customers want too!

So why, when I say "thank you" to a cashier, do I get that proverbial deer-in-the-headlight look like I'm speaking a foreign language that they don't understand?

And … why am I – the customer – the one saying "thank you"?

Here's a fun little game. Go to a store. Purchase something. Wait for the cashier to say "there you go" while giving you a receipt. Look at the cashier. Say "thank you." Watch what happens.

My guess is that the cashier will stumble through a confused "you're welcome" and then move on to the next customer.

When did customer communication move into Backward Land? Why am I, the customer, thanking the business for allowing me to spend my money there? And when did "there you go" become an acceptable replacement for "thank you"?

Train your team (and yourself) to say the words "thank you."

Seriously. 2 little syllables. They carry tremendous power in your customer communications.

Please and thank you go a long way

True story:

Went through a fast food drive-through. While waiting at the window for my food – after a very pleasant greeting of "$9.71" (and literally no other words) from the restaurant's employee – I noticed a sign behind him. Actually, it was more of a scrawled message on a whiteboard, but I took it as a sign.

The message said, "Please and thank you go a long way." YES! At last, I'd found a store manager who had it right.

Alas, the employee returned – after a very long, lonely absence – and handed me my food. "Have a nice day" was all I got. Okay, so that's polite and nice and all, but I seriously doubt it was anywhere close to sincere.

I had to ask. And I did, as pleasantly and in as good a humor as I could muster. "That sign behind you – is that for employees to read or just something nice for customers to see?" The employee was absolutely, positively dumbfounded. It was as if he was seeing that message for the very first time. I'm guessing that was the case, actually.

He asked me – and I am NOT making this up – "You want me to say please and thank you?"

Seriously? Yes, dear, I am your customer. I just handed you money. (Remember the "$9.71"?) You could say thank you.

That's not really what I said in response, of course. My even smarter response was "Yes. It goes a long way," as I again pointed to the sign.

The employee gave a bit of an embarrassed giggle but still did not get it. After a moment's pause, I said "thank you." Twice. He said ... wait for it ... "you're welcome."

So I gestured. No, not that kind of gesture. I gave him a visual signal that I expected HIM to say "thank you." And hooray! He did actually say it. Although, again, I seriously doubt it was anywhere close to sincere.

Please and thank you ... they do go a long way ... when they are used! These words have magical powers. They can make customers happy, convince customers you honestly appreciate their business, and bring those customers back for more.

Somewhere along the line we have lost our basic manners, in our lives and in our businesses. How often are you, as a customer, handed a receipt with a hearty "here you go"? Are you, the customer, the one who always says "thank you" to the person who just took your money?

Or maybe that "here you go" was not so hearty. Maybe it's more like "I have a job that pays less than what I deserve and I'm just ready for my shift to be over so here you go."

Don't get me wrong. I feel for people who are not making what they should and who are in jobs that are nowhere near their career choice. However, regardless of what job they (we) do, they (we) need to put heart and manners into it.

As a business owner, you need to be sure your employees are doing just that. Customer communications can make or break your business. If a customer is already disgruntled, the lack of communication on your employee's part can send that customer packing.

Pleasantries, those basic manners, can defuse a potentially catastrophic situation for your business and may even give you one more happy customer. If your customer is already satisfied with your business, those magic words will just add to their loyalty.

Write great sayings on a whiteboard, but make sure your employees actually see the signs and follow through. Train your employees on effective customer communications that include the need to say "please" and "thank you" frequently. It will go a long way – for your customers and your business.

Employees can learn. Customers can be more appreciated. All it takes is an extra breath and another two words: "Here you go. Thank you!"

Your turn

Do you use your words for good? Think about the times, over the past week or the past month, that you have forgotten your basic manners. Note those incidents here.

Now, what can you do to ensure that you use your words for good going forward, with:

- Co-workers

- Bosses and employees

- Vendors

- Customers

◻ ◻ ◻

In the virtual world, remember the humans!

Social media is easy

It's ridiculously easy to post in the virtual world, isn't it? Whip out that phone, hit a few buttons, and your message is there for anyone and everyone to see.

Okay, who am I kidding – your phone's been in your hand the whole time.

Convenience aside, the part that's not easy about social media is thinking about who that "anyone and everyone" might be and how they'll react to your virtual words.

Stories abound of "accidental" posts, in which personal information or offensive messages are sent out for the world to see. Venting on a faceless forum is easy. Guess who is on the other side of that faceless forum? Yes, you've figured it out by now. Those are humans. They could be co-workers, bosses, or even (gasp!) customers.

Before hitting that post or send or whatever key, think about the faces of the actual human beings who will read your words. How will they take your message? Sometimes the answer to that is easy.

If you're writing something offensive, it's a safe bet they'll be offended. Even if you think your words are innocent enough, though, they could be misinterpreted.

Tread carefully through social media in the business world. Words on a screen are never just words on a screen. They will be read by ... you got it ... humans.

JK doesn't always cut it

In the world of social media, mistakes can be fixed with a simple jk – just kidding. Or can they?

Once the words are out there, they're out there for good. First impressions have been made. Quite possibly, feelings have been hurt. Even more possibly, clients have been lost if the words have not been chosen carefully, with humans in mind.

There are emojis that help explain laughter or sorrow, but emojis are not really appropriate for business use. There is text language to modify messages, but text language is not generally appropriate for business use.

So, when you've posted or sent a message that was misinterpreted, adding a smiley face and a jk doesn't really cut it in the business world (or anywhere else for that matter).

Choose your words carefully, think about the humans on the receiving end, and then craft a message that will not offend, be misinterpreted, or send a client packing.

Faceless forums all have faces on the reading / viewing end. Write for those faces, not from your own emotions.

And now for something a little different

For your amusement (and shock and horror?), some real-life examples of unwise social media posts, from entrepreneur.com and pcmag.com:

"Bragging about a job offer on Twitter and insulting the company that offered you said job is not a smart move. A 22-year-old recent grad with a degree in information management (ahem), found that out the hard way.

"After being offered a position from California tech company Cisco in 2009, Riley tweeted:

"'Cisco just offered me a job! Now I have to weigh the utility of a fatty paycheck against the daily commute to San Jose and hating the work.'

"Her tweet elicited a huge response on Twitter -- including from a Cisco associate who responded he'd be happy to pass her sentiments on to HR. Suffice it to say, her job offer disappeared."

(entrepreneur.com – March 2016:
https://www.entrepreneur.com/article/271823)

After the 2017 Boston Marathon, Adidas "tweeted out, 'Congrats, you survived the Boston Marathon!' inadvertently recalling imagery of the 2013 Boston Marathon bombing. The company recovered swiftly by immediately taking the tweet down and issuing a heartfelt apology."

(entrepreneur.com – May 2017:
https://www.entrepreneur.com/article/294925)

"… the Department of Education sent out a tweet misspelling W. E. B. DuBois's name, then misspelled 'apologies' as 'apologizes' in its follow-up apology-for-misspelling tweet."

(entrepreneur.com – May 2017:
https://www.entrepreneur.com/article/294925)

"T-Mobile Austria stepped in deep security doodie when replying to a user on Twitter who asked if it stores passwords in clear text. The answer: *Yes*. Plus, customer service could see part of each password! It even added, 'I really do not get why this is a problem.' Of course, security-wise, it's a huge problem. Three days later, the company changed its policy and took steps to secure all passwords."

(pcmag.com – April 2018: https://www.pcmag.com/feature/335422/19-massive-corporate-social-media-horror-stories/1)

If you wouldn't say it in person, to an actual human, don't say it in the virtual world.

Your turn

How many times have you posted something and then immediately wished you hadn't?

Have you ever lost a client or offended a co-worker because of social media?

What can you do to help ensure your social media messages will not be misinterpreted or offend other humans?

❐ ❐ ❐

And, in conclusion . . .

No time?

"If you don't have time to do it right,
when will you have time to do it over?"

~*John Wooden*

You don't have time for training. But, do you have time to compensate for and correct all the mistakes made when there has been no training? How much time does it take to apologize to clients for employees' lack of customer service or communication skills?

You don't have time to update your website. But, do you have time to explain to potential clients why the content on your website has not changed since you launched your business? How much time does it take to explain that you don't have time to post relevant, helpful information that your clients could use?

You don't have time to learn how to communicate more effectively. But, do you have time to clarify misunderstood messages or clean up messes created by miscommunication? How much time do you spend emailing back and forth, trying to explain the first email? How much time do you spend expressing regret for messages that shouldn't have been delivered or that were delivered to the wrong people?

Time is an investment in your organization's success. Take the time to think about your audience, your message, and your intent when preparing your communication pieces. Take the time to ensure your communication is clear and concise – and understood correctly by the correct recipient.

Take the time to review and update your content, whether it appears on your website, on promotional material, or on the front wall of your office.

Take the time to train your staff on communication skills.

Proper workplace communication requires that investment of time, so you won't waste time explaining yourself or correcting mistakes later. At that point, it will probably be too late.

Business secret: Communicate often – and well

I didn't know.

My manager didn't tell me.

That's the first I've heard of it.

That clerk was so rude. I'm never going back there again.

Those people don't seem to talk to each other.

Sound familiar? Are people saying this in or about your business?

Communications can help or hurt your business. Poor – or no – communications actually can cost your business. Communications with customers are especially crucial, but even internal communications can significantly impact your business success.

Let's start with the last couple of comments above. What are your customers / clients saying about your team members? Do you have a rude employee? Do you have employees who clearly want to be somewhere else, in the midst of a customer transaction?

I've seen fast food employees checking their cell phones as they were taking orders from customers. I've been on the receiving end of a very rude company representative who was obviously ready to go home when I expected a certain level of customer service toward the end of his work day. I've also had extremely pleasant exchanges with a clerk in a grocery store. Guess which business I will recommend to others and return to on a regular basis?

Internally, your employees may be repeating the first three comments above. Managers have their meetings and then go about their business without sharing vital information with their team. Individuals working on a project find it easier just to do the work alone, rather than involve co-workers. Front-line employees don't get the information that is decided behind closed management doors.

I've worked in a corporate environment that was so stressful, we were standing in line hoping for our turn when the layoffs started. Most of the stress was caused by communication issues. There was virtually no downstream communication. Mistakes were made because people did not have the right information or, in some cases, any information.

Your secret to business success? Communicate with your customers. Communicate internally. Do it often. Do it well. Misinterpretation can be just as harmful as no communication.

Remember they are all humans.

Write your emails so they are clearly understood, without a long chain of follow-up messages. Make a phone call to discuss things. Make meetings meaningful by providing actual information and answering questions.

Of course it will take some effort. If it were easy, everybody would be doing it! Train your team members to understand what your customers need to know and to learn how to provide that information to them on a regular basis.

Train your managers to consider what their team members need to know and to learn how to provide that information to them on a regular basis.

Communication can hurt or help your business. Clear, regular communication can be the secret to your business demise or to your business success.

Talk to me like I'm a human.

Your turn

It's all up to you now. What lessons have you learned here?

What can you immediately put to use in your business or your job that will make a difference in your communication?

Now that you have all this amazing information – and your astute notes – how will you make you sure you are communicating with others as humans (even when you're convinced they just landed from Mars)?

❏ ❏ ❏

In conclusion (for real, this time)

Now that you've read through these words of wisdom, I can tell you that it takes being exposed to 91 pages of tips, guidance, stories of experience and lessons learned, and pages designed for your own input, to "get" the message about communicating with other humans … as humans.

So, put it down and look up. Talk to the humans in the room with you. The virtual world can wait.

Thanks for reading.

❒ ❒ ❒ ❒